TREKKING on a TRAIL

Hiking Adventures for Kids

LINDA WHITE

Illustrated by Fran Lee

GIBBS·SMITH
P
PUBLISHER

Salt Lake City

This is a Gibbs Smith Junior book, published by
Gibbs Smith, Publisher
P.O. Box 667
Layton, Utah 84041

To order: (1-800) 748-5439
Website: www.gibbs-smith.com

Edited by Suzanne Taylor
Designed by Fran Lee
Manufactured in Hong Kong in July 2016 by Paramount Printing Company Ltd

NOTE: Some of the activities suggested in this book require adult assistance and super-vision, as noted throughout. The publisher and author assume no responsibility for any damages or injuries incurred while performing any of the activities in this book. DISCLAIMER: The publisher and author warn that there is inherent danger in the activity of hiking and that children should always be supervised by a responsible adult when hiking. The publisher and author bear no responsibility or liability for injuries or property damage that may result from hiking or participating in any activities described in this book.

Library of Congress Cataloging-in-Publication Data
White, Linda, 1948-
   Trekking on a trail : hiking adventures for kids / Linda White;
   illustrated by Fran Lee.
      p. cm.
   Summary: Discusses various aspects of hiking, including warming up, gear, packing, safety, map reading, food, topography, and more.
   ISBN 10:0-87905-941-9 ISBN 13:987-0-87905-941-5
      1. Hiking for children—Juvenile literature. [1. Hiking.] I. Lee, Fran, ill. II. Title
GV199.54 .W55 2000
796.51—dc21
                                                                    99-038486

To a generation of Trekkers:
For Son Ryan, who has trekked the globe
and found adventure, understanding,
and a packsack full of memories;
Nephew James, who did trek the desert
where he tested his strength and
endurance and won;
Nephew Ezra, who trekked to
mountaintops where he witnessed
fireworks, both natural and manmade.
—LW

For my doggie-boy, Travis,
my all-time favorite trekking partner.
—FL

Contents

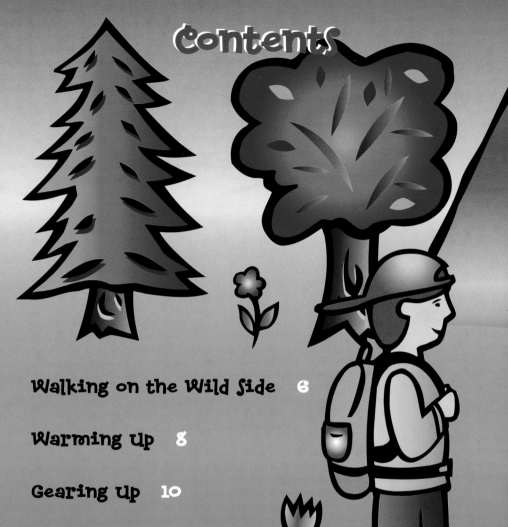

Walking on the Wild Side

WOULD YOU LIKE to go somewhere you've never been, do something differ-ent, see new places, but don't have transportation? Look down—the answer could be dangling at the ends of your legs—your own two feet. Why not take a hike?!

Hiking is different from just plain walking. Hiking is adventure. It takes you to places where no roads go, to mountaintops where you can see for-ever, to cooling streams teeming with aquatic life, to caves that are home to fish with no eyes, to prairies and grasslands where you might see prairie dogs or foxes.

As with most outdoor activities that take you away from home, hiking is more fun if you've done a little preparation.

This book helps prepare you well for your adventure. You'll do a few exercises to ready your body, assemble some basic equipment, pack a bit of hiker grub and a map, and out the door you'll go. Rikki Raccoon will tramp along the trail with you, offering tips and crafty hiker activities.

You can do much of the planning and preparation by yourself, but when you near the time to set out, it's time to get your parent or other adult helper involved. Talk about the hike you want to take, review your preparations, and find a time when they can go with you. Kids should <u>always</u> hike with an adult. Along the trail, you'll be making memories together that you'll talk about for a long time to come.

Can you hear the outdoors calling? Wonders await. Let's take a hike!

Warming Up

WHETHER YOU SET out on a short or all-day hike, hiking is more than walking.

Most people are in physical shape for hiking short distances. But stronger legs are needed for walking up and down hills, and stronger arms and shoulders for carrying a pack loaded with gear.

For those longer hikes, you may want to shape up a bit. Any physical activity you do beyond what you usually do will condition your body.

Here are a few stretches to limber you up. Do them before and after your other physical activities.

Peeping Owl Plant your feet shoulder-width apart and bend your knees. Turn your head slowly to the right and try to peer over your right shoulder. Next, turn your head slowly to the left and peek over your left shoulder. Do this five times, s-l-o-w-l-y.

Rubber Wings Place your feet shoulder-width apart and bend your knees slightly. Reach behind your head and put one hand between your shoulder blades. With the other hand, pull your elbow back. Hold that position for fifteen seconds. Do the same thing with the other arm.

Crumpled Crane Sit on the floor with one leg straight out in front of you, your toes pointing up. Bend the other leg and put that foot against the straight knee (your bent knee will rest on the floor). Lean forward, reaching for your toes with both hands. Hold for fifteen seconds. Repeat with the other leg straight. Do this five times.

Grounded Butterfly While sitting, put the soles of your feet together and clasp your ankles. Pull them toward you while your elbows rest on your knees. Hold for fifteen seconds.

Boulder Roll Stand facing a wall with one foot ahead of the other. Place your hands against the wall at shoulder height. Bend the front knee and keep back knee straight. Lean forward until you feel the stretch in your back leg. Hold fifteen seconds. Don't bounce. Repeat with other foot forward. Do both five times.

Gearing Up

ARE YOU GOING for an hour-long hike along the beach or a two-day winter hike in the mountains? The trappings you pack depend on where you are going and how long you'll be gone. In any case, remember:

- Anything you take, you carry.
- Pack as little as possible.
- Don't forget the necessities.
- Make sure everything you take is lightweight. Your pack will be much lighter, and on the trail, you'll be glad it is!

Choosing Basic Stuff

You'll need the following items for most hikes.

Clothing

Choose layers of extra clothes to put on or take off as the weather changes. Two layers are enough for most summer hikes. Take more if the weather is unsettled because you'll be hiking during cool and hot parts of the day.

◎ Tops [T-shirt, flannel shirt, fleece shirt, lightweight jacket, coat with hood]
◎ Bottoms [shorts, loose-fitting cotton or nylon pants, fleece pants, insulated pants]
◎ Head [hats for warm weather (with a brim to protect you from the sun) and/or cold weather (with a brim plus ear covers)]
◎ Hands [gloves or mittens (essential for cold weather)]

Footwear

If your feet aren't happy, the trail will be a miserable place. A hiker with sore feet whines and limps and slows the hike to a stop.

The most important essential for happy feet is comfortable shoes or hiking boots that support your feet and ankles. You must be able to walk all day without rubbing blisters on your feet. Hiking boots are the best footwear for the trail. However, kids have growing feet and hiking boots are expensive. If your everyday athletic shoes fit well and are sturdy, they should work for most hiking.

If you'll hike often or in rugged or rocky terrain, hiking boots could prove a sound investment. When you buy hiking boots, go to a reputable outdoor shop. Ask questions and try on many pairs.

Break-in is the process of getting the boots to fit your feet comfortably. Wearing stiff new shoes or boots for an hour or so a day "breaks down" the material. It softens and begins to fold in the same places your foot does. Do this every day until your boots feel foot-friendly. Never wear shoes or boots on the trail until you've broken them in.

Socks Don't wear all-cotton socks when hiking. They absorb moisture and encourage blisters. Part wool or all wool is best. If shopping for boots, wear the socks you will wear on the trail, usually a pair of thin socks with a pair of heavier socks over them.

Gear

Make sure you have these things with you on any hike:

- map/trail guide—get two: 1) pack one, and 2) leave an extra with a responsible person back home. Trace your route on it and note the time you expect to be home.
- pocketknife (USE A SHARP KNIFE ONLY WITH AN ADULT'S PERMISSION)
- compass
- lip balm
- sunglasses
- sunscreen/sunblock
- first-aid kit
- plastic bags (small, self-sealing)
- trash bags
- flashlight/batteries
- whistle
- watch
- matches
- coins
- toilet paper

Food

- water
- lunch
- snacks

Gear & Food

Asking Rikki about Water

Can I drink from the stream?
No. Water is often polluted by users upstream from you. Besides, it's home (and bathroom) to fish, beaver, and other critters.

How much water do I need?
In hot weather, half a quart for each mile you hike. In cold weather, half a pint for each mile you hike.

Why the difference?
You lose more water through perspiration in hot weather than you do in cold weather. What you lose must be replaced.

How should I carry my water?
Carry it in a plastic container with a top that closes tightly. You may want one large bottle or two smaller ones. Some hikers like containers that hook onto a belt while others prefer one on a strap to loop across their body. Some models have hooks and straps and can be carried either way. There are even soft water carriers you wear on your back. They come with a long straw so you can slurp cold water as you tramp along the trail.

Help! I'm going on a long hike and can't carry that much water. You say I shouldn't drink the river water. What do I do?
Water tablets and portable water filters are available at outdoor and sports shops. Use them to treat river or stream water. They clean the bad stuff out, making the water safe to drink. Ask the salesclerk to show you how they work.

Packing Up

NOW YOU"VE GOT your gear together, will you have to juggle it along the trail? Of course not. You'll carry all that paraphernalia in a pack. They come in several sizes and styles to suit different needs.

Fanny packs clip around your waist and have enough room for only a few items. Use one when taking a short hike.

Day packs are carried on your back and are large enough to carry the needs of a full day.

Backpacks are a larger version of the day pack. Built on a metal framework, there's room in them to pack enough for trips that will last more than one day.

Planning for Weight

How many pounds should you carry in your pack? A growing kid shouldn't lug more than 20 percent of his or her body weight. To find out how much that is, divide your weight by five. Example: If you weigh sixty pounds, divide that by five.

A sixty-pound person should limit their gear (including pack) to twelve pounds. What's your limit?

When full, this pack weighs 12 pounds.

Looking for Features

If you are purchasing new equipment, tell the clerk at the outdoor shop what kind of hiking you plan to do. He or she will be able to show you several pack models that are right for your needs, explain their features, and fit the pack to you.

Search for these features:
- padded shoulder straps
- padded back
- reinforced stitching
- smooth-working zippers covered with a flap
- sturdy, waterproof, rip-resistant fabric
- outside compartments
- two-layered pack bottom
- the right size for your use
- waist straps on day packs; waist and chest straps on backpacks
- reflector strips

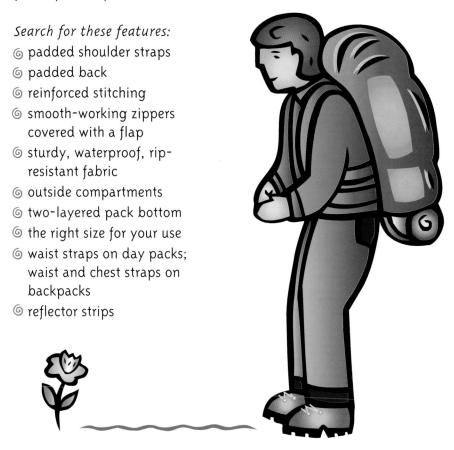

Ask the salesperson to load up the packs you are trying to decide between with a load similar in weight to what you'll carry on the trail. Try out each pack. Wear it around the store. See which feels best. Tell the clerk about any problems. Sometimes a simple strap adjustment will make a world of difference.

Wising Up

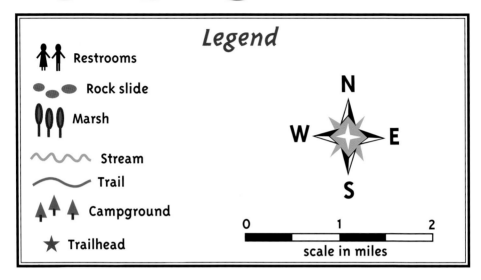

Legend

👭 Restrooms

⬬⬬ Rock slide

▮▮▮ Marsh

〜〜〜 Stream

〜〜 Trail

🌲🌲🌲 Campground

★ Trailhead

N
W ✴ E
S

0   1   2
scale in miles

THE MORE YOU KNOW about hiking, the more you'll enjoy it. The following are things you should know before heading for the trailhead.

Reading a Map

You'll find there are many kinds of maps, but you'll want to locate a trail map at a bookstore, recreation center, outdoor shop, or park-service information station. Once you have a trail map, review it. Is there a creek along your path? How far is it to the cave you've heard about? How long would it take you to get there? Answers to these questions can be found on the Legend.

The Legend contains the map's scale, the directional compass, and the symbol library.

What's the scale? The scale is how much real space is represented on the map. If one mile of real distance is represented by three inches on the map, you can measure the trail you want to take.

If, on the map, the trail is six inches long, and three inches represents one mile, then how long is the trail? (Answer: two miles)

The directional compass shows you which way north, south, east, and west are on the map. North is usually at the top of the map.

The symbol library explains what each symbol on the map means. From it, you can figure out which line is a road, a trail, or a stream, where the campgrounds are, and, just in case you need one, the location of the nearest rest room. It will also indicate the trailhead, which is where the trail begins.

1. How far is it from the trailhead to Twin Owls Rock?
2. Do you cross a stream, a marsh, or a rock slide when walking from Mount Casper to Gold Rush Gulch?
3. Is Sun Rise Campground closer to Rainbow Pond or Twin Owls Rock?
4. If you are at Big Bear Cave, how far is it to the nearest rest room?
5. If you are at Gold Rush Gulch and your car is parked at the Shaggy Moose parking lot, what direction do you walk to get there?

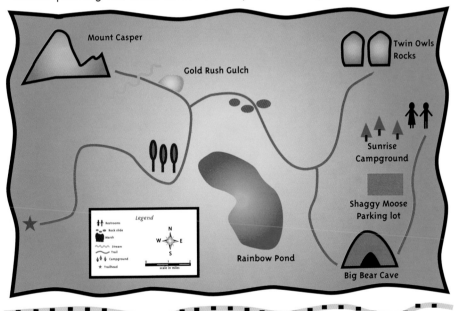

Lay a piece of string along the scale of your map. Using a marker, mark the string at each half-mile mark. Now you can lay the string on the map along the part of the trail you want to hike and figure out about how far your walk will be. Pack the string with your map.

Playing It Safe

Hey, there are no doctors' offices in the wilderness. If you get hurt, it could take a while to get you back to town. It's best to take extra care not to get into dangerous situations. Stay away from drop-offs, learn to avoid the poisonous plants that grow in your area, and stay off slippery rocks, especially those near fast-moving water. There's plenty of fun to be had without taking unnecessary risk.

Staying Found

Being lost in the forest is no fun. There are no street signs or familiar buildings to help you get back to camp, and one tree can look pretty much like another.

Here are some simple things that will help you stay found when hiking:

1. Always let someone know where you are going and when you'll be back.
2. Never hike alone.
3. Stay on trails.
4. Pay attention to the land you are walking through. Turn around occasionally and look behind you so you'll know what to look for on the way back. Watch for landmarks: bent trees, oddly shaped rocks, caves, or trees that have fallen across a stream.
5. Carry a whistle and a mirror.

   a. If you get lost, blow the whistle three short bursts every few minutes, then listen. The whistle can be heard much farther than your voice can.

   b. Flash the mirror in the sunlight, especially if you are high on a hill. It can be seen for many miles.

6. Carry an area map with you. Before setting out, sit down with your adult and look at the map. Locate roads, rivers, forests, and any landmarks you can see. On the trail, turn the map so that those map markers line up with what you see. Mark the trail you are going to follow.
7. Always carry extra water and snacks with you. If you do get lost, you'll be a lot more comfortable while you wait to be found.

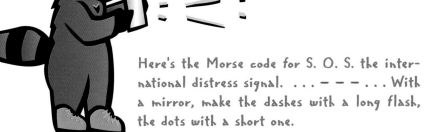

Here's the Morse code for S. O. S. the international distress signal. ... − − − ... With a mirror, make the dashes with a long flash, the dots with a short one.

Help! I'm Lost!

First of all, stay calm and stay where you are!

You will be tempted to try to find your own way out, but if you are scared, you may trek miles off the course. Your fellow campers will look for you in the area they think you went, so hug a tree and stay put. Blow your whistle in a series of three blows every few minutes until you are found.

If you must leave the area to climb a tree or nearby hill to signal with your mirror, mark your trail so you can get back and others will know how to find you.

If you end up spending the night, look for a natural shelter. It might be an overhanging rock or bushes that form a curve. You can make a simple lean-to shelter using dental floss and a solar blanket. Put the back of the lean-to into the wind.

Crafty Hiker: Emergency Kit

In a self-sealing plastic bag, assemble all of the things you might need in an emergency.

whistle (you can wear it around your neck)

map

shatterproof metal mirror

solar blanket

10 feet of bright-colored plastic tape

matches/strike strip in a waterproof container

firestarters

dental floss

candy bar

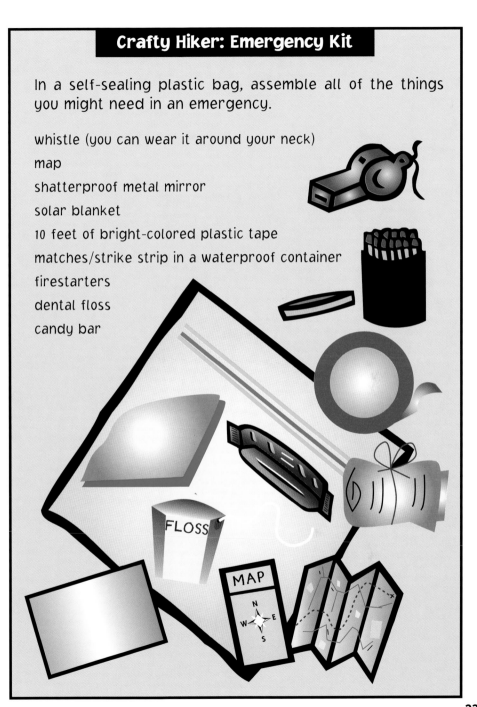

Reading the Weather

Bad weather can turn you from a happy hiker into a damp duck in just a few minutes. Experienced hikers keep an eye on the weather. They start watching the forecast days before their hike and keep watching the sky for clues to possible weather changes while they are walking. Moody weather doesn't necessarily mean you must cancel your trip. Many people prefer hiking in a drizzle to hiking in the hot sunshine. It just means you must be prepared and take enough gear to protect yourself.

Weather Signs for Hikers

If you notice these, put on your boots. The weather should be good for being outdoors.

1. A mellow, yellow sunset or sunrise.
2. A gentle wind.
3. No clouds, high clouds, thin clouds, or few clouds.
4. A clear blue sky.

Be careful in sunny weather. Too much of a good thing can leave you looking like a lobster and acting like a crab. Remember to wear sunscreen.

But, if you see these things, consider staying home with a good book.

1. A red sunrise.
2. A sudden drop in temperature.
3. Increasing winds.
4. Low clouds, dark clouds, or fast-moving clouds.
5. A ring around the sun or moon.

"Red sky at night, sailors delight,
Red sky in morning, sailors take warning."

Lightning

Beware of lightning. It could be a shocking experience. If it begins while you are out, don't keep walking. Find a place to wait until it moves away. You'll be tempted to get under a big tree, but, since lightning strikes the tallest things in the area, that is actually a dangerous place to be. The best place is on the ground in the open. Don't sit or lie down, but squat. If you were to be hit, the lightning would travel from your legs and feet into the ground, protecting your vital organs.

Applying First Aid

Your first-aid kit contains everything you need to doctor little cuts, bumps, bruises, and especially blisters! If you stumble into a gopher hole and twist your ankle, get ambushed by a tree, or grow a blister from hiking all the way to a cave and back, you'll be able to clean the body part and ease the pain if you have the following things packed in a small container or sealable plastic bag.

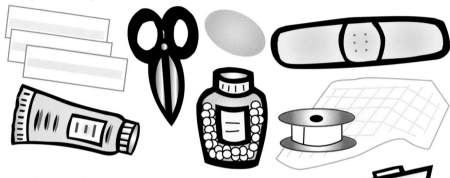

- moist towelettes
- bandages
- gauze and adhesive tape
- moleskin
- small scissors
- aspirin or other fever and pain reducer
- antibiotic cream

Your adult should have a first-aid kit, too, to doctor bigger hurts.

The American Red Cross, schools, hospitals, and other organizations offer first-aid classes. You'd be smart to take one before hittin' the trail. Some outdoor shops also offer outdoor first-aid and wilderness-survival classes.

For "Hot Dogs"!

It pays to be aware of your "doggies" (feet). You can learn to prevent most blisters. While hiking, if you feel a spot on your foot getting hot, stop. Your foot is being rubbed raw. If it continues, a blister could form. Just cut a piece of moleskin a little bigger than the sore spot and stick it over the area. The soft moleskin will probably prevent a blister, and you'll walk a lot more comfortably.

If you already have a blister, don't pop it. Cover it with moleskin that has a small hole cut to fit over the blister, or cover it with a bandage; leave it until the body re-absorbs the fluid. If the blister does rupture, keep it clean so it won't become infected. Wash it with mild soap and water, then bandage it. If a blister becomes red, a doctor should look at it.

After hiking all day, coddle your feet with a warm-water bath. Then dry them well, especially between those tootsies. Put fresh moleskin or bandages on any sore places. Cover with clean cotton socks.

Ahhh, that feels good.

Weather-Related

Let's face it. When any person—young or old, male or female—gets too hot, they sweat. Sweat evaporates and cools the skin. Sweat is a loss of fluid. If fluids aren't replaced, sweating decreases and the body gets hotter.

Heat exhaustion has the following symptoms: you feel faint and sick to your stomach, your skin is pale and clammy, and you have a headache or feel weak. What should you do? Stop walking, lie down in the shade, put your feet up, rest, and drink water. If you have salt with you, put a little in your water. The water will lower your internal temperature. When you feel better, start back. Keep replenishing your body fluids by drinking water. It would be a good idea to see a doctor when you get back to civilization.

Environment-Related

Bugs

The best thing to do about bugs is to avoid them. That's not so easy when you are hiking around in their living room. Bees, yellow jackets, and wasps usually bug you just when you annoy them, but ticks and mosquitoes think you are dinner delivered on a hiking boot. No time outdoors will be free of bugs unless you are hiking in the snow. So, what should you do?

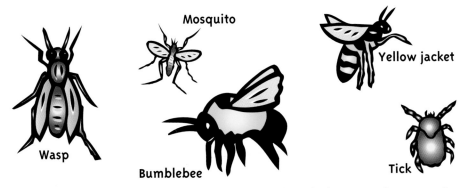

Mosquito

Yellow jacket

Wasp

Bumblebee

Tick

1. Dress for bug defense—Wear long pants and tuck them into heavy socks. Fashion goes out the window when it competes with pesky bugs. You can also wear a lightweight shirt with long sleeves to protect your arms. Dark clothes attract insects so wear light colors.

2. Wear insect repellent—The most effective insect repellents contain a chemical known as DEET. If you use these, follow the directions on the container. Keep DEET-containing solutions tightly closed, sealed in a sealable plastic bag, and carried in a separate pocket of your pack. They can melt down some plastics and will ruin your camera.

Many people are allergic to DEET or don't want to use chemicals. There are natural bug foils like citronella oil that can be used. They are not usually as effective as DEET but still offer some resistance.

3. Treat bug bites—Baking soda mixed with a little water is a lightweight itch stop for mosquito bites and you can use it for toothpaste, too. But don't use it on bee or wasp stings. They need something acidic like lemon juice. There are also some easy-traveling sticks of stop-itch available as well as the traditional calamine lotion.

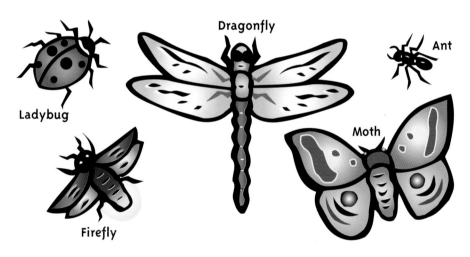

Dragonfly

Ant

Ladybug

Moth

Firefly

Enjoy the insects you see from afar. Can you remember their names and colors?

Insects are more aggressive in the evening than in the morning. So remember: early to bed, early to rise, makes hikers less itchy and a lot more wise.

Tick, Tick, Tick

Ticks are plentiful in many areas. They are small eight-legged bugs with hard flat bodies. They bite and suck blood and can also transmit such diseases as Rocky Mountain spotted fever and Lyme disease. Both of these can be treated, but you are better off to try to avoid them. Wear insect repellent and dress for bug defense. Occasionally, check your clothing and flick off any ticks you find. If one latches onto your skin, remove it—all of it—with a pair of tweezers, being careful not to squash the tick. When you get home after hiking in tick country, have someone check through your hair and on your scalp for ticks. You can check your body. Check especially in tight dark places like armpits and groin. If rashes, headaches, fever, or severe muscle aches develop a few days after hiking, head for the doctor for some tick treatment. Be sure to tell him or her you were in a "ticky" area.

Poisonous Plants

One of the main reasons people hike is to enjoy nature. But, not all of nature is so enjoyable—there are poisonous plants that can drive a hiker wild. A hiker who brushes past poison ivy, poison oak, or poison sumac may not even notice . . . until twenty-four to forty-eight hours later. That's when the itchy, blistery, red rash shows up. Avoiding these villainous bushes is the best defense. Watch out for these and step around them.

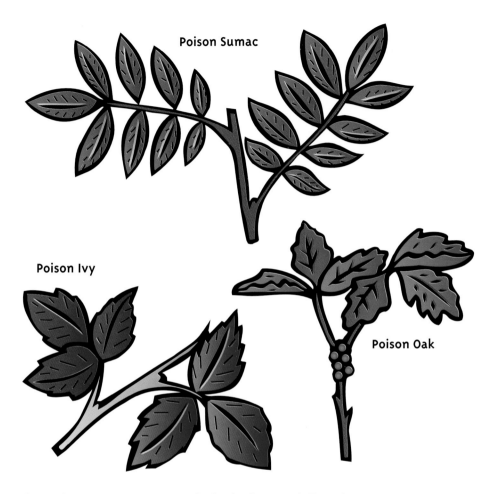

Poison Sumac

Poison Ivy

Poison Oak

If you do come in contact with the bad guys, follow these steps:

1. Wash the plant's oils off of you as soon as possible. Remove and wash clothing that may have contacted the plant also, handling it as little as possible.
2. Clean the contaminated skin area with alcohol. There are individually packaged alcohol-soaked towelettes available.
3. When a rash develops, dab with calamine lotion.

Filling Up

YOU'RE NOT LIKELY TO FIND a hamburger stand or take-out pizza along the trail. So, if you think you'll get hungry while on your hike, you'd better take food with you. At the very least, take something to nibble on in case you aren't able to get back when you planned.

Here's a list of great grub for the trail and some recipes that will keep you searching for a shady spot for a rest stop.

Choosing Trail Grub

Any of the following food items will pack well and satisfy your hunger.
• Dried fruits
• Nuts
• Hard-boiled eggs
• Sandwich foods—peanut butter, cheese, canned
   meats or fish
• Whole-grain breads and foods
• Cookies
• Instant fruit juices
• Fresh fruits and vegetables

Save the extra vacuum-sealed condiments from a fast-food visit. Bacteria can't get into the factory-sealed pouches so you can take things that would ordinarily need to be refrigerated, like mayonnaise. There are packaged salad dressings to use with fresh vegetable sticks. Mustard, honey, and jelly also come in pouches or tubs and might be a welcome addition to your outdoor lunch.

Making Trail Treats

These recipes are easy to make and delicious to eat or nibble on.

Peppermint Orange Juice

no cooking/1 serving

What you need:

1 orange (Valencia oranges best)
1 peppermint stick

What you do:

1. Roll the orange on the picnic table to loosen the juice.
2. With a small knife, cut a cone-shaped hole in one end of the orange.
3. Put the candy stick in the hole.
4. Bite the end off the candy stick and suck on it as you would a straw. It may take a little while to get the juice started.

G.O.R.P.
(Good Old Raisins and Peanuts)

mix at home/serves many

What you need:

2 cups roasted peanuts

½ cup raisins

1 cup of any of these: chocolate candies, licorice bits, chocolate chips,
nuts, seeds, dried fruit, pretzels, sesame sticks, dry cereal

What you do:

1. Pour ingredients into a half-gallon sealable plastic bag; mix.
2. Pack in small pocket-sized bags to take along on the trail.

Peanut Butter Logs

mix at home/makes 8 quarter-cup servings

What you need:

½ cup peanut butter
½ cup dry milk powder
½ cup honey
1 tablespoon cocoa powder
¼ cup chopped nuts
¼ cup raisins
¼ cup coconut (optional)

What you do:

1. Dump all ingredients into a one-quart sealable plastic bag.
2. Squeeze bag gently until all ingredients are mixed.
3. Divide mixture into eight equal pieces.
4. Roll each piece into a log.
5. Wrap each log in plastic wrap.

Trail Dust

What you need:

6 cups multigrain Chex cereal
1 cup peanuts or mixed nuts
1 cup small pretzels
1 cup bite-sized bagel chips
¼ cup butter
1 tablespoon Worcestershire sauce
¾ teaspoon salt
½ teaspoon garlic powder
¼ teaspoon onion powder

What you do:

1. Heat oven to 250 degrees.
2. Melt butter in a baking pan in the oven.
3. Stir in all seasonings.
4. Stir in all other ingredients.
5. Mix until all ingredients are evenly coated.
6. Bake 45 minutes, stirring every 15 minutes.
7. Spread on paper towels to cool.
8. Put one cup of mixture in each of nine self-sealing, pint plastic bags.

Trekking the Trail

WELL YOU'VE WARMED UP, geared up, wised up, packed up, and filled up. Finally, you're ready to take a hike. What will you see? Whether you hike in the forest, the desert, or near a swamp, you're sure to see many wonders of nature.

As you go on your first hike, don't rush. Walk at a leisurely pace. You'll soon fall into a comfortable stride. This first hike might be just to observe. Take in the sights, sounds, and smells of the area. What do you see? At each place you hike, you will see different things.

Watch for bird nests, snake skins, feathers, nursery logs, mushrooms, fish, animal tracks. Soon you'll realize that much of the fun of hiking is in studying nature and much of the fun of studying nature is in the detective work. Who made these tracks? What kind of bird dropped this feather? Every good detective takes notes.

How about making a hiking journal for your trek? You can include notes on the date of the hike, weather conditions, where you are going, and a diagram of the landscape. Sketch the animal tracks you see along the creek, add a feather you found, draw the tadpole you saw in the big puddle. Maybe later you can find out how long it will be before the tadpole becomes a frog. You can also add photographs from your hike—like the chipmunk that chattered at you while you ate lunch, and one of your big brother when he fell in the creek.

Crafty Hiker: Hiking Journal

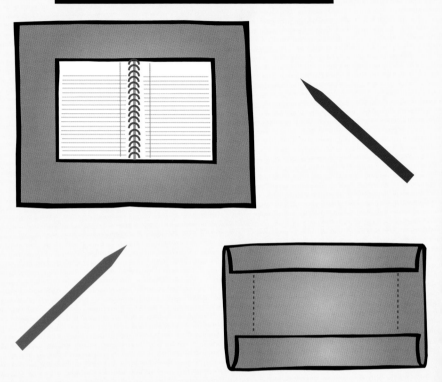

A hiking journal can be as simple as a pocket-sized spiral notebook with a pencil attached to it by a cord. But if you cover it like you might cover a school book, with paper cut from a brown paper bag, you can decorate the journal with your favorite hiking memories.

1. Cut a piece of heavy brown paper bag or decorative paper six inches wider and six inches taller than your opened notebook.

2. Place opened notebook on the paper so there is about the same amount of paper showing on the top and bottom and on each side.

3. Mark the paper along the top and bottom of the notebook.

4. Fold the top down and the bottom up along the lines you just marked. Your paper should now be the same height as your notebook.

5. Curl the last three inches of one side forward and insert the notebook cover into the flaps created at the top and bottom. Fold neatly and tape the cover flap to the cover at the top and bottom. Do the same with the other side.

6. Decorate with markers, crayons, colored pencils, or watercolors. It's hard to decide on a design. You could draw a mountain sunset, a rainbow trout, or an odorific skunk chasing a bear. Can't decide? Make several.

Crafty Hiker: Hiking Stick

A hiking stick gives you something to lean on when the trail is steep or rocky, steadies you when you cross a stream, and provides something to hang onto at the end of the day when you are too pooped to go any farther.

1. Select a straight sturdy stick about shoulder height.
2. If you want, peel off the bark carefully. Cut away from your body, watching out for your knees.
3. Wrap the grip area with a soft leather strip to cushion your hand. Tuck ends under the wrapped strip.
4. Personalize your stick by adding designs with markers or paint or by carving patterns. Be careful.

When people share the woods with bears, one can scare the other. When hiking in bear country, it's a good idea to whistle, talk in a loud voice that can be heard a long distance, or carry a walking stick adorned with jangling bells. With a little warning, bears have a chance to depart before you even know they were there.

To make your walking stick a bear stick, tie three or four loud bells onto a cord or leather boot string. Wrap that around the grip of the stick and tie securely.

Getting Acquainted with Nature

Tracking is following an animal's
tracks, hoping to find the animal.
When they are bear tracks,
I go the other way.

Animals

When hiking any trail, you'll probably wonder whose home you are tromping through. You may not see many animals at first. They are expert listeners and sniffers and make a hasty departure when they know others are coming their way. You can find out who lives there. Use your detective skills. Animals leave telltale signs and you can learn to read many of them.

A good place to find signs is along a riverbank or lakeshore. Most animals go there for water sometime during the day, usually at dawn and dusk. When they do, they leave something behind—tracks.

A deer's track is different from that of a squirrel, a beaver, or a bear. Compare these tracks to the ones you see and find out who's been there. Some animals leave tail or wing prints, too. And most animals leave scat (poop).

Deer

Rabbit

Dog

Squirrel

Fox

Chipmunk

What if you want to see the animal, not just the tracks? There are two ways:

1. Sit very still. Watch and wait. You'll be surprised how much you really do see.

2. Track the animal. Before you do, make very sure it's an animal you want to find. You'll be happier when you suddenly come upon a squirrel, rabbit, or fox than if you crest a hill and find yourself face-to-face with a skunk, porcupine, or hungry bear. You'll enjoy watching them much better from a safe distance. That doesn't have to be from inside your car.

Here's how you track animals:

1. Make as little sound as possible. Unfamiliar sounds frighten away

Skunk

Raccoon

Beaver

Porcupine

Bear

animals. To walk silently on hard ground, put your toes down first. On soft ground, heels go down first.

2. Walk into the wind so your scent will be carried away from the animal, not toward it. Unfamiliar scents frighten away animals.

3. Learn what animals eat. If the animal you want to see is a berry eater, don't look for it in the willows. If it eats fish, you could be wasting your time looking for it on the side of a hill.

You'll find many other signs left by animals—nests, burrows and mounds, stripped pine cones, tree bark gnawed or peeled away, tree trunks felled by chewing, branches nibbled, grass flattened. Who or what do you think did these things? Why? How? You'll never get bored hiking. There are too many mysteries to solve.

Crafty Hiker: Sooperdooper Outdoor Snooper Kit

How big is that track? What is that bug carrying? What kind of fur is caught on that branch? Along the trail you're going to see things you want to know more about. It's good to have some tools to help you out. Put these things in a large self-sealing plastic bag.

What you need:

Magnifying glass

Ruler

Tweezers

Pocket-sized field guide

Sketch pad/pencil/colored pencils

Bug jar

Add one or more of the following items. Before packing them, remember: they are going to seem a lot heavier at the end of the day.

Small camera

Binoculars

Tape recorder

Crafty Hiker: Bug Jug

What you need:

Small plastic jar

Small plastic magnifying glass

Scissors

Craft knife

Hammer and nail

White glue

What you do:

1. Cut a hole in the jar's lid slightly smaller than the magnifying glass. You may find it helpful to make a circle of holes first, using the hammer and nail, then cut between the nail holes with a craft knife to make the large hole. Ask your adult helper to assist with this.

2. Make five or six air holes in the lid or jar using the hammer and nail.

3. Glue the magnifying glass onto the lid so it covers the large hole.

4. Find an insect to study. Look under logs, rocks, or leaves. Be sure to set the bug free when you are finished looking at it. Don't keep it more than a few hours.

A word about collecting: In days of yore, like when your parents were young, people hauled rocks, feathers, bird nests, and other things home and made collections. Today, we know that these things are all a part of the land and are more valuable where they are than in the bottom of your closet. Now, collecting is done more with pictures, drawings, and memories. Keep a photo album, sketch pad, scrapbook, and hiking journal as your collection. Stack them neatly on a shelf where you can find them.

Birds

A bird is a bird is a bird, right? Wrong. Though all adult birds have feathers, there are birds that fly and birds that can't. Some birds sip nectar from flowers, others crush seeds for the food stored inside, and even more nab insects, catch fish, or consume carcasses of unfortunate animals. Some roost on tree branches, others in hollow trees, while several burrow in the ground. Hummingbirds are so small, their babies could fit in a thimble. But an ostrich, at eight feet tall and over three hundred pounds, is big enough for a grown person to ride.

You can learn a lot by just looking at a particular bird. Sketch it in your hiking journal so you can identify it later. Be sure to note the size you think it is and the color of its plumage. Look at its beak. Did you know you can tell what type food it eats by the shape of its bill?

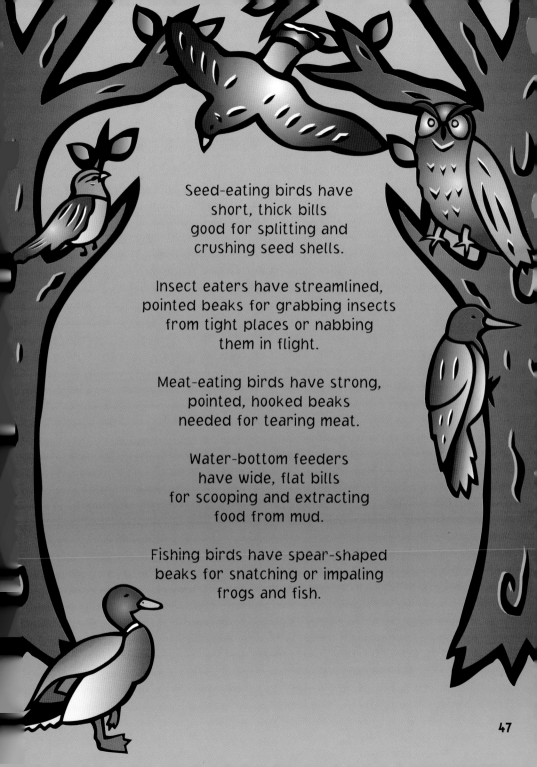

Seed-eating birds have
short, thick bills
good for splitting and
crushing seed shells.

Insect eaters have streamlined,
pointed beaks for grabbing insects
from tight places or nabbing
them in flight.

Meat-eating birds have strong,
pointed, hooked beaks
needed for tearing meat.

Water-bottom feeders
have wide, flat bills
for scooping and extracting
food from mud.

Fishing birds have spear-shaped
beaks for snatching or impaling
frogs and fish.

Perching feet are small and agile for holding onto branches.

Wading feet are long and skinny to keep the bird from sinking in mud.

Swimming feet are webbed for pushing against water like paddles.

Clutching feet are powerful with sharp, curved talons for holding onto prey.

Crafty Hiker: Bird-Hike Record

Set aside one hike to just learn about birds. Before you go, learn to identify the birds in your area by their call. Take plenty of paper and colored pencils. Draw all the birds you see in one hour, one bird on each sheet of paper.

Ask someone to take your picture or a picture of everyone with you.

When you get home, use a bird guidebook to identify the birds you saw. On one sheet of paper, write down some interesting facts about each bird. Do they live in your area all year or do they leave during the winter or summer? How many eggs do they lay? What does their nest look like? Which ones are swimmers, perchers, predators? What type of bill do they have? What do they eat? Does the male or female sit on the nest? Who feeds the babies?

When you have learned all you can about the birds, stack the sheets together, with the picture of a bird followed by the information you have learned. On an extra sheet, write a little about your hike. Write down all the things you want to remember. Tell who went with you, what day you went, where you went, and what you saw.

On yet another sheet of paper, glue the picture that was taken of you or your group. Add a title like "My Bird Hike" or "On the Trail of Little Birdie Feet," your name, and date of the hike. Once you attach a colorful cover—maybe a tree full of birds drawn on bright construction paper—you have a wonderful keepsake of your hike.

Plants

Plants are important! Some hikers think plants are the least interesting part of being outdoors. After all, they don't run or swim, chirp or growl. Plants just stand there waving in the breeze. But, what would your hiking area look like without them? You'd sit in the broiling sun to eat lunch rather than in the shade. There'd be no animals to watch because there would be no nuts, cones, berries, or greens to draw them there. Rain would wash away the hillsides with no roots to hold the soil in place. And everything would be the color of the dirt.

Pick only a few leaves or flowers if you need them for a project. The plant needs most of them to make food for itself and the creatures who live near-by, and to attract pollinators. Leave plants rooted in the ground so they can keep growing.

Ask permission before picking leaves or flowers. It's against the rules to pick any living thing in many wilderness areas.

Never eat anything you find growing along the trail. Unless you know exactly what you are eating, you could get pretty sick. Many poisonous berries look a lot like the tasty ones.

Take time to enjoy the many varieties of plants around you—trees that lose their leaves and those that don't, plants that have flowers and those with cones, ferns that are found in moist places, and mosses that grow on rocks. What else can you find?

Study plants. They are more interesting if you know about them. Look for something amazing about each one.

Crafty Hiker: Textured Paper

August, 12

Many people have done rubbings of leaves, but did you know you can make rubbings of other things as well? Want to remember the unusual tree bark? Do you really like the texture of a rock? Want to make a border of grass blades on a page of your journal to remember a special picnic spot? Make a rubbing.

What you need:

hiking journal or other paper

pencil/crayon

DAD

In the Woods

In the woods
there were trees
and rocks.
The grass felt
so good,
I took off
my socks.

What you do:

1. Lay one sheet of your open journal or other paper on the tree trunk or whatever texture you want to rub.

2. Using the side of your pencil or crayon, gently rub it back and forth on your paper over the texture you want to capture.

3. Try making a border of one texture around another texture. Use that special page for something you want to highlight—a poem about the place you made the rubbings, a photograph, or something important to you.

Use this same technique to make special note cards, wrapping paper, or bookmarks. What else can you think of?

Rocks

Rocks can be a towering perch for peering into the next county or even state. Rocks can be a spot to sit while you dangle your tired feet in the cool water. Rocks can be stacked to mark your trail. Rocks can make a pleasing kersplash when you skip them over the water. Teeny, tiny rocks make up the sand you squish between your toes.

Rocks are not all the same. And they change. Big rocks become little rocks, little rocks become sand. They don't change enough in a day or a year or maybe even a lifetime for us to notice, but they change. They are worn down by wind and rain, broken apart by fire and ice, carved by rushing river waters and crashing ocean waves.

Skipping Rocks Across Water

Don't expect to skip a rock the first time you try—maybe not even the hundredth time you try. But, don't give up. Once you can make it skip one time, try for two, then three. Some people can make one rock skip more than twenty times before it sinks.

- Gather a handful of flat, round rocks about the size of a small pancake.
- Hold one between your thumb and forefinger, with your index finger wrapped around the rock's edge.
- With your palm up and the rock flat, swing your arm back.
- Bring your arm forward quickly, flick your wrist, and allow the rock to spin off the end of your index finger.

Rikki's Junior Ranger Trailside Quest

Want to see how much you've learned? Play this wilderness scavenger hunt. Find everything on the list, and be sure to keep track of bonus points you earn. Leave everything where you found it so the next hikers can play, too!

Pinecone (1)

Leaves (3 shapes): +2 bonus points for each one identified

Rocks (3 types): +2 bonus points for each one identified

Birds (3 kinds): +2 bonus points for each nest (don't touch!)
+10 bonus points for identifying a bird call

Insects (3 kinds): 3 bonus points for each one identified

Rodents (2)

Trees (3 kinds)

Animals (3): +5 bonus points for finding tracks
+5 bonus points for identifying tracks

Leaving No Trace

Put together all the living things that are together in one place and you have what is called an ecosystem. Different plants and animals grow in different ecosystems. Cactus and lizards are at home in the dry heat of the desert, but polar bears and low-growing alpine plants prefer the cold, wind-swept tundra.

Whatever ecosystem you get to hike in, remember, it's somebody's home. Treat it better than you would your own, and help keep the wilderness you hike in wild.

◎ If you pack it in, pack it out. Keep a small bag in your pack for litter. You can dispose of it properly at home.

Always expect the unexpected

- Stay on established trails.
- Leave logs, rocks, dirt, and plants where they are. You came to visit nature—leave it natural.
- Use "the rest room" far away from bodies of water. Otherwise, human waste will be washed into the water with the next rain. Those wastes are harmful to the fish who live there and to the animals and humans who live downstream.
- Leave the trail better than you found it. If you see someone else's litter alongside the trail, pack it out too. You shouldn't have to, but you'll be glad you did.

Checking your Packing List

AS YOU PLAN your hike, check off each of these items when it is ready to pack:

◎ **Day pack/fanny pack**
◎ **Water/water container**
◎ **Food**

◎ **Clothing**
       shirts/jackets
       pants
       sturdy shoes
       thick/thin socks
       hat
       gloves/mittens

◎ **Sunglasses**
◎ **Sunscreen/sunblock**
◎ **Flashlight and batteries/bulb (extra needed)**
◎ **Watch**

◎ **Emergency kit**
       trail map/guide
       whistle
       shatterproof metal mirror
       solar blanket
       bright plastic tape (10 feet)

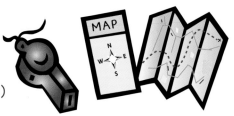

matches/strike strip in waterproof container
firestarters
dental floss
candy bar

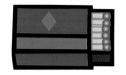

◎ First-aid kit

moist towelettes
bandages
gauze/adhesive tape
moleskin
small scissors
aspirin/other fever-and-pain reducer
antibiotic cream
baking soda

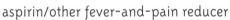

◎ Optional items

plastic bags (large/small)
toilet paper
hiking journal
camera/film
binoculars
cell phone (for emergencies)

detective kit:
magnifying glass
ruler
field guide
sketch pad/pencils
bug jar
casting material
small camera
binoculars
tape recorder

Learning More

AS YOU SPEND more and more time on the trail, your list of questions will grow. How was this land formed? How did the mountains get so high? Why is the lake so deep here? What is the altitude? How does that affect what grows here? What birds live here? Do they live here all year long or are they seasonal? Do the trees here lose their leaves in the winter or are they evergreen?

Where would you look to find the answers?

Trail and nature guides about your area offer the most specific information. These are available in bookstores, nature centers, and recreation, park, and forest-service offices.

Encyclopedias offer a wealth of information on such general subjects as deer, cedar trees, or rocks.

Libraries have hundreds of books to keep you reading about all the trail subjects that stir your interest. Look in the nonfiction section of your library. Books are arranged by the numbers printed on their spines. Those numbers correspond to subjects. If you have questions or need help finding something, your librarian will be happy to help you.

Seeking the Pros

Organizations

National Audubon Society
700 Broadway
New York, New York 10003
(212) 979-3000
www.audubon.org

Boy Scouts of America
P.O. Box 152079
Irving, Texas 75015-2079
(214) 580-2000
www.bsa.scouting.org

Girl Scouts of the USA
420 Fifth Avenue
New York, New York 10018-2798
(800) 247-8319
www.gsusa.org

Campfire Boys and Girls
4601 Madison Avenue
Kansas City, Missouri 64112-1278
(816) 756-1950
www.campfire.org

American Red Cross
Public Inquiry Office
11th Floor
1621 N. Kent Street
Arlington, Virginia 22209
(703) 248-4222
www.RedCross.org

Outdoor Shops

Eddie Bauer
P.O. Box 182639
Columbus, Ohio 43218-2639
(800) 426-8020
www.eddiebauer.com

Eastern Mountain Sports
327 Jaffrey Road
Petersborough,
New Hampshire 03458
www.emsonline.com

L.L. Bean
Freeport, Maine 04033
(800) 341-4341
www.llbean.com

R. E. I.
1700 - 45th Street
Sumner, Washington 98390
www.rei.com

Collect them all!

Salt Lake City